MATH ALL AROUND YOU

written by Michael Burgan

illustrated by Michael DiGiorgio

TABLE OF CONTENTS — PAGE

McGraw-Hill School Division

New York Farmington

THE SHAPES AROUND US

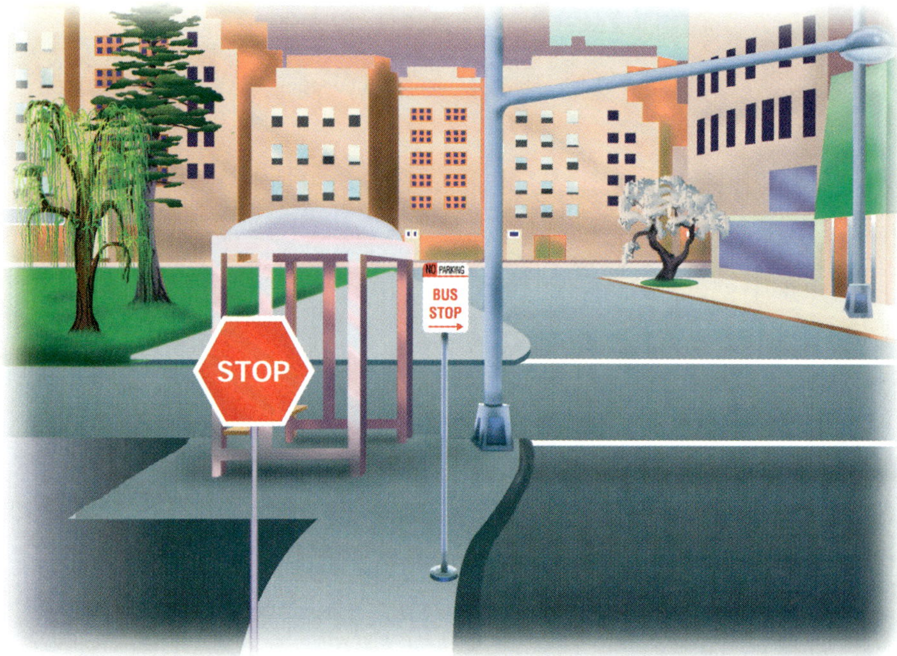

Take a walk outside. If you look carefully, you will see shapes and patterns all around you. Some of them have been created by people. A building might be in the shape of a cube. Road signs come in all shapes: circles, rectangles, triangles. On a highway, you will see a pattern of broken white lines used to separate the lanes. A pattern on clothing might have crossing lines of different thickness that form tiny squares.

Shapes and patterns of all kinds also appear in nature. The first humans probably learned about shapes and patterns by observing the plants and animals around them. You might not realize it, but those natural patterns and shapes have something to do with math.

Of course, you don't see numbers scattered all across the landscape when you go outside. And animals can't do multiplication tables or long division—at least not as far as we know! Yet the natural world offers examples of some of the ideas mathematicians have studied for thousands of years.

KEPLER'S DISCOVERY

Johannes Kepler, a German astronomer made an important discovery in the 17th century. After years of studying the position of the planets, Kepler found that a numerical pattern existed. He made up an equation involving the distance of a planet from the sun, and the revolution of that planet—that is, the time it takes a planet to orbit the sun. When Kepler plugged the numbers into his equation, he made a strange discovery. For each planet, the final number was always the same. Kepler had found a relationship between the position of the planets, though he didn't know what to make of this pattern. This pattern is now known as Kepler's Third Law of Planetary Motion.

In his studies, Kepler also noticed that the path of any planet around the sun formed a special figure: an oval shape called an *ellipse*. Before Kepler, scientists assumed a planet's orbit was a circle.

Kepler also looked at much smaller shapes and patterns. He believed that snowflakes were made up of tiny particles of the same shape packed together to form the flake. He based this on his observation that a snowflake has symmetry.

Something with symmetry has balance. If you split a square down the middle and fold it over, each half exactly overlaps the other. The halves are mirror images of each other. This is called symmetry. A snowflake has six identical arms that stem from its center. This kind of symmetry is called rotational. If you rotate a flake around the center, it always looks the same.

Science has shown that Kepler was right. A microscope reveals that a snowflake is made up of tiny six-sided snow crystals. These crystals form a symmetrical shape with six points. Every snowflake is unique, but they all share symmetry.

Symmetry appears often in nature. Starfish, which usually have five arms, are symmetrical. Raindrops are symmetrical spheres as they fall through the sky.

Viruses, tiny creatures that can spread disease, come in symmetrical shapes. One of the more common shapes is an *icosahedron*. This shape is made up of 20 equal triangles. If you've ever had chicken pox, then you've had an icosahedron-shaped virus inside of you! It's another example of nature's symmetry. (Though it's probably no comfort to know something so balanced can trifle with your health!)

The icosahedron is one of the more unusual shapes found in nature. As you might guess, you have to look very hard to find it. No one can see a virus without a microscope. Other shapes might also be hard to detect with the naked eye. If you cut through a gem called tourmaline, you'll see many triangles, one inside the other. And using a microscope will show you that tiny salt crystals, like the ones you put on food, come in the shape of cubes.

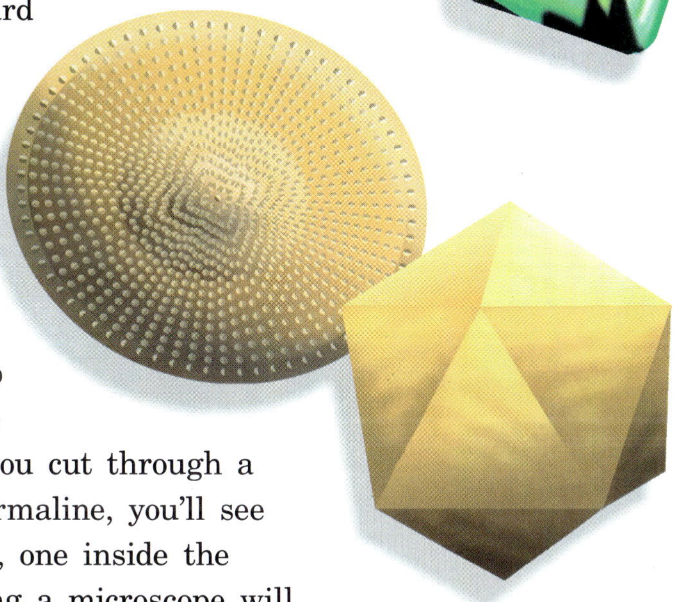

Other shapes are easier to see. Cut down a tree and you can see the rings—circles—that mark its age. Watch a raindrop hit a pond and you see rings again. These are waves created by the raindrop.

HEXAGONS AND SPIRALS

Another geometric shape you may have already detected in nature is the six-sided *hexagon.* Some hexagons, such as ice crystals, can't be seen without a microscope. But if you've ever seen a honeycomb, you know it's packed with little sections where bees store their honey—each of these sections is a hexagon. By instinct, honeybees build the combs with this shape. The repeated pattern of hexagons offers the most storage space in a compact area.

Bees use geometric shapes in another important way. You may have heard of the bee "dance." When a bee finds a source of food, it returns to the hive and dances for the other bees. This dance tells the bees where the food is located. Scientists now know that the dance follows a definite geometric pattern. The bee that has found the food makes a short run, shaking its body as it does. Then it turns to the left or right and walks in an arc back to where it started. The bee does the shaking run again, then walks back on the opposite side in another half-circle.

Through its dance, the bee duplicates the exact angle of the hive from the source of the food. Other shapes in the dance tell the bees how far the food is from the hive.

Another shape often found in nature is the *spiral.* A spiral is a type of curved line. When water goes down the drain of sink, it spins in the shape of spiral. A spiral that has three dimensions—height, length, and depth—is called a *helix.*

Spirals can be huge. Our solar system—Earth, the sun, and the other planets—is part of a larger system called a galaxy. Pictures taken from space have shown that our galaxy, the Milky Way, is in the form of a spiral. Another large spiral is the shape of a hurricane. When seen from space, this type of storm moves as a spinning spiral. A body of water can also form smaller spirals called whirlpools. The spinning motion of the water pulls in any objects nearby.

One natural spiral has fascinated mathematicians for a long time. This spiral is the "home" of a tiny sea creature called the *nautilus,* which is related to the snail. Like a snail, the nautilus has a shell, and as the nautilus grows, its shell grows too. Over time, each new section of the shell forms a spiral. Cutting the shell in half shows the individual sections.

Spiral patterns are also found in flowers and other types of plant life. The buds of morning glories are spiral-shaped. Over time, however, the spirals unfurl as the flowers bloom.

If you look at a daisy, you'll see it has tiny dots on its head. These dots are called *florets*. The florets spiral out from the center toward the edge. If you look very closely, you'll see there are actually two sets of spirals. One turns clockwise and the other turns counterclockwise.

Other plants have two sets of spirals. The scales on pinecones and the bumps on pineapples have similar patterns of clockwise and counterclockwise spirals.

FIBONACCI'S SEQUENCE

Over time, scientists discovered that the number of florets and scales in these different spirals often match a number in a special numerical sequence. The sequence is: 1, 2, 3, 5, 8, 13, 21, 34, 55 . . . . Can you see the pattern in this sequence? Starting with 3, every number in the sequence is the sum of the two numbers before it. This sequence is called the Fibonacci sequence. It's named for the 13th century Italian mathematician who discovered it.

An interesting thing about the Fibonacci numbers is the ratio between the neighbors in the sequence. After 3, the numbers form a ratio of about 1:1.6 Try it for yourself and see. If you divide 8 by 5, the answer is 1.6. Twenty-one divided by 13 is 1.615. Fifty-five divided by 34 is 1.617. You can do this for any two numbers in the sequence and the answer will always be very close to 1.618.

The number 1.618 was already special to mathematicians in Fibonacci's time. It was the so-called "Golden Section" or "Golden Ratio." Scientists had already discovered that this ratio appeared in nature. Engineers often used it when they designed buildings. A structure that had a 1:1.6 ratio between its height and length was thought to be more pleasing to look at than any other ratio.

Like the spirals in daisies, many other plants also have Fibonacci numbers for their petals or leaves. Lilies have three petals, buttercups have five, delphiniums have eight, marigolds have 13. The spirals on daisies usually have 21 and 34 florets. The seeds in a sunflower also form a spiral pattern, and the number of seeds in each spiral is usually a Fibonacci number.

Over time, scientists became fascinated with the appearance of number patterns in plants. In the 18th century, two mathematicians first noticed the spiral pattern in pinecones. In the next century, two brothers named Bravais measured the angles formed by seeds in their spirals. They discovered the angle was usually 137.5 degrees. This angle appeared so often, it was called the Golden Angle. This angle was related to the "Golden Number," 0.618034. This number is the result when you divide 1 by the Golden Section, 1.618.

In the 20th century, scientists finally began to understand why nature favored the Golden Angle for aligning seeds and florets. The greatest number of seeds that can be packed into a flower head occurs when the seeds form spirals with an angle of 137.5 degrees. This tight packing of seeds helps make the plant strong. More experiments showed that the seeds have to emerge in this tight spiral pattern—it is simply how plants are meant to grow.

Studying plants and how they grow has led to another mathematical discovery. Think of how a tree grows. An individual branch comes out of the main trunk of a tree. Over time, the branch looks like the tree it grew out of, and then this branch has more branches growing out of it. These branches also develop the same basic shape of the tree itself. A geometric shape that repeats over and over within an object is called a *fractal*. In nature, the shapes might not be exact, but they are close. Scientists can create exact fractals using mathematical formulas and computers. The resulting shapes have many jagged edges that are repeated endlessly. These images are sometimes considered art.

Scientists have also turned deep inside the human body to see the role of mathematics there. This study has shown that the tiniest cells have geometric shapes, and their actions are ruled by laws of physics and chemistry that can be explained in mathematical ways.

Your body is made up of more than one trillion (1,000,000,000,000) cells. Each cell has to be able to move. Proteins in the cell help create this movement. Two specific proteins, called *alpha-tubulin* and *beta-tubulin*, come together to form thin tubes. These tubes are symmetrical. One scientist compares them to brick chimneys.

Imagine the alpha-tubulin are white bricks and the beta-tubulin are black ones. The first layer of the protein chimney alternates one white brick and one black. In the second row, a white brick sits on top of a black and a black sits on top of a white. This pattern is repeated all the way up the chimney. Then, many of these cylinder-shaped chimneys join together. The cell uses these tubes to search for food. If the cell finds food, it makes a bigger protein chimney, which helps pull the cell toward the food. All this occurs with complex mathematical rules at work.

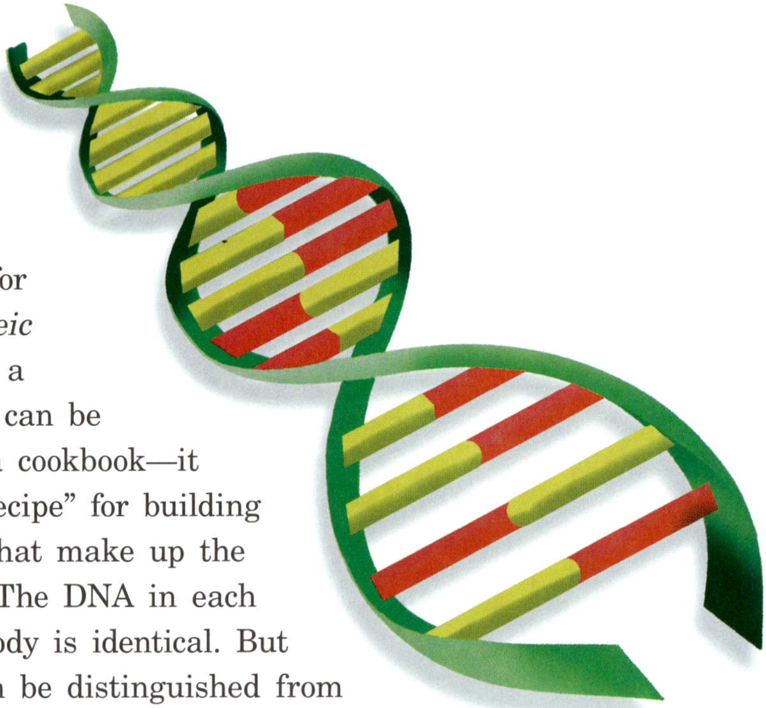

Another tiny part of a cell is DNA. (This stands for *deoxyribonucleic acid.*) DNA is a chemical that can be compared to a cookbook—it carries the "recipe" for building the proteins that make up the human body. The DNA in each cell of your body is identical. But your DNA can be distinguished from the DNA of anyone else on Earth. The odds of two people (who are not identical twins) having the same DNA are 1 in 3 million.

In 1953, scientists proposed a model of what DNA looks like. We now know that DNA forms in the shape of a double helix. You might recall that a helix is a spiral that exists in three dimensions. The DNA double helix is like a twisted ladder. Each spiral is connected with "steps" that are made up of chemicals called *bases.* Each step is made of a combination of two bases. Finding the pattern of these bases helps scientists understand the recipe in the DNA.

From the path of planets to the cells in your body, mathematical shapes and patterns are always at work. You never know where you're going to find nature's math.